Living Happily
Ever After

Living Happily Ever After

Bob Mumford

Spire BOOKS

FLEMING H. REVELL COMPANY
Old Tappan, New Jersey

Library of Congress Cataloging in Publication Data

Mumford, Bob.
    Living happily ever after.

    1. Marriage. 2. Conduct of life. I. Title.
HQ734.M885   261.8'34'2   73-4607

ISBN 0-8007-8151-1

Contents

Introduction

Love, it seems, is serious business. It has a way, as well, of being extremely demanding. In the following pages we shall recognize the seriousness of love and marriage, but—hopefully—add to the length and duration of your joy and happiness. This can be done only by fulfilling the demands of love as they appear on the horizon of life. A happy marriage means security, fulfillment, and above all, the ability to cope with the demands of your mate.

I have endeavored to keep this presentation short and simple. It is my intent that we avoid the dos and don'ts of marital conduct. If you can grasp *three basic principles* as given here, you will find that they are workable in any marriage. Remember, proper conduct usually follows correct attitude.

Finally, we make no apologies for personal illustrations. That is what marriage is all about.

> God, our Father, grant that through these pages the reader may be given insight into the mystery of a man with a maid—in Jesus' Name—Amen.

Bob Mumford

I
The Blessing
of Incompatibility

Most people get married—some more than once —but how many couples do you know who are genuinely happy together? Divorce courts are jammed, marriage counselors work overtime and many so-called experts question seriously if the institution of marriage will survive. Consequently, many couples are experimenting with other kinds of relationships. Even though the odds against marriage as a satisfactory way of life sometimes appear overwhelming, I am convinced that marriage is meant to work. The problem is *not* with the institution of marriage, but with the *people* in it. Most of us simply do not know *how* it is supposed to function.

"How tos" are important in every area of operation. In this case, it isn't that we are left without advice, information, or warnings! Libraries carry many volumes on the subject. Bookstands overflow with helps priced from forty-nine cents to ten dollars and forty-nine cents. Almost every current magazine carries an article about marriage. There is even computer service designed to locate the perfect mate for you. With all of these so-called aids, why do so many marriages still fail? I believe there is only one answer to our world-wide dilemma, and for it we must go back to the origin of marriage itself and take a look at the *Manufacturer's Handbook.*

As a matter or presupposition, I must state frankly that I believe God created man and woman, and His intention was for them to be *one* in marriage. *How* this is to be accomplished is fully explained in the Bible, which is our *Handbook* for daily Christian living. To the readers who disagree with me in this, I must also say that I have no helpful suggestions about how to live happily in marriage *apart* from God's framework and prescription. In fact, I don't think it can be done. In this book we are going to be discussing marriage from that vantage point.

Our subject is so complex, intricate, and personal, that anyone who approaches it as "an authority" is taking on quite an assignment! I choose to bring my thoughts to you simply as one man desiring to share three basic principles which over the past ten years have not only revolutionized my own marriage, but proved invaluable—as well as valid—in counseling others in theirs.

First, let me say that I believe our homes are under satanic attack. There is a calculated design against this institution of marriage—a diabolical desire to bring division between husband and wife. Satan is aware of the strength to be found in unity between these two. He realizes that this bond represents a great mystery—a spiritual secret that can virtually force him out of business! And the pressures of our society are going to become so strong that only the husband and wife who have found a satisfactory answer will be able to withstand the onslaught—sexually, emotionally, financially, morally, spiritually.

Frightening? Yes—but *you* can be part of the answer. It is God's prerogative to begin revision and revolution in this area of His creation with whichever member of the marriage union He chooses. He will

12

begin with the one who is listening. Will you open your ears as you read? It works better, of course, when both marriage partners are willing to sit down and study the *Manufacturer's Handbook* together. But God can move with definite assurance in any situation.

The origin and nature of marriage as presented in the Bible is pictured in these three excerpts:

> And the Lord God said, "It isn't good for man to be alone; I will make a companion for him, a helper suited to his needs" . . . This explains why a man leaves his father and mother and is joined to his wife in such a way that the two become one person.
>
> Genesis 2:18,24

> . . . a man should leave his father and mother, and be forever united to his wife. The two shall become one—no longer two, but one! And no man may divorce [or separate] what God has joined together.
>
> Matthew 19:5,6

Or to put it another way, "The woman was created to meet man's needs and in marriage the two are to become one person." (See Ephesians 5:31.)

We see that in Genesis God explained just what His intention was in uniting man and woman into one unit of society. Jesus quoted this passage from Genesis to His disciples, stressing the intended permanency of God's original plan. Paul also repeated this intention in writing to the Early Church.

Centuries of trial and error seem to focus our attention on one particular word at which we shall take a long look—*incompatibility!* For one of our anniversaries my wife gave me a contemporary greeting card which said: YOU FURNISH THE INCOME AND I'LL BE 'PATIBLE.'

A couple, divorced after twelve years of marriage, said, "We studied books on marriage, consulted experts, tried group therapy, and in the end the strain became so bad we had to get divorced to keep from hurting the children any more than they already were." Then these two became Christians, discovered that God had a perfect plan for marriage, and were remarried in church. After a few years they stated they had never been happier in their entire lives!

"The secret was in letting God make the two of us one," they confided. "Two human beings can never—on their own—become one, no matter how hard they try. But when they both submit to God, He will make them one, and their marriage is as solid as a rock. The difference in our two marriages can be compared with night and day—or better still—hell and heaven!"

This brief testimony of divorce could be repeated thousands of times but the resolution of it not quite so often. Divorce—with its anger, pain, and personal injury—is seldom an answer. Rather it is a temporary relief from the symptoms of a disease which was never diagnosed—let alone treated. Also, many people will bear witness to the fact that if you can't make the first one work, the odds against the second one being successful are much higher.

What is the source of conflict which causes divorce when often neither of the couple really desires it? Why should marriage in our day be looked upon as something to be avoided? In the multitude of reasons we find selfishness, in-laws, environment, religious differences, finances—and on and on we could go! Man seeks for more than the basic animal needs of life—food, sex, and self-defense. Security, adventure, recognition, and love by common consent enter into his needs. Why, then, cannot the science of social behavior, marriage data processes, the present sexual revolution—or even personal preference—guarantee one success in the marital bond?

We mentioned briefly computer service selection available to prospective brides and grooms. When the data input is complete, one is to find the perfect mate —chosen because of the same views on children, money, and social values. Two people discover they are very much alike in their desires for recreation— both like the color blue and quiet songs. Education, environmental, and religious similarities all line up to "prove" this must be a successful marriage. Eighteen months later these two find they just cannot stand each other! If there are children, they decide "to stick it out for their sakes." If religious and social pressures are sufficient, an intricate facade may be erected that few can penetrate. You know, we can become masters at hiding the depth of pain experienced by our being *forced* on each other due to an institution called marriage. If our morals are high, we may even be denied the sexual satisfaction we need so badly. Then there is the possibility of the extramarital affair with its hurt and far-reaching implications. What modern technology had promised would be workable because two were so perfectly matched turns out to be just another wreck on the mounting pile of casualties.

If two who are seemingly compatible can't make it

in the land of "happily ever after," what about the two who have differences right from the beginning? What hope is there for them? Their song goes something like this: "The day we met we knew we couldn't stay apart—but every time we come together there is tension, problems, and disagreement. We can't get along with each other—or without!"

2
Human Inadequacies

One plus one equals one! That equation just doesn't figure, does it? Both Einstein and any child's kindergarten teacher would agree that it cannot be a correct answer. But the Divine Mathematician says that's the way it is in marriage. He who designed the product ought to know the solution to the problem. He ought to be able to be aware of the hazards—furnish the missing parts—recommend the necessary adjustments to guarantee smooth performance.

While I was studying psychology, one of my professors came out with this startling statement: "In human experience no man or woman is an adequate and total personality in himself." When I first heard this it was a horrible blow to my male ego. Then I thought, "I know why—sin came into the world." But God seemed to say, "Oh, no—not because sin came into the world. Think again. . . ." Could this possibly be the answer to the failure of the computer and its unsatisfactory output? Was it that there was nothing wrong with the computer, but that man-made machines just were not destined to come up with spiritual equations? Was God all the time standing over the sophisticated attempt, saying, "I didn't make marriage to work that way. Why don't you try Me?"

Is it possible that God, in His creative processes, actually formed the human personality in such a manner as to leave *him* and *her* inadequate? Only with biblical presuppositions could a person even *think* this way. For me there began unfolding a principle which has proved itself over and over again. Incompatibility is just a refined way of saying, "We are just too different—we just cannot get along together." Is this really grounds for divorce or the touchstone of unity? So we need to find out *why* disagreement exists and *how* it is to be resolved. The *Manufacturer's Handbook* is very explicit on these two issues.

God designed marriage to bring to man and woman the ultimate in blessings. In one place He speaks of it as "heaven on earth." In order for this to be accomplished, God says in effect, "When I made man, I only made a half. Then when he meets his mate, he meets the other half." That which is inadequate in itself must have these "missing parts" supplied if happiness is to result. Are lights beginning to go on for you? Perhaps picturing the principle will be a help.

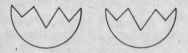

These constitute two identical halves—each inadequate and incomplete in itself. No chance of these two ever making one complete whole.

A continual attempt to find supply and adequacy in one's self, or in another of a different sex—even though like you—results in friction and frustration. If marriage is to supply your needs, it cannot be that two identical halves be joined.

18

When we are joined to our "true love," it usually is one who is quite different in temperament. We may like many of the same things (externals), but in personality (the internals) we are very different. The basic observation is this: God creates us with inadequacies, both male and female, but when the two meet, true adequacy *may* be achieved. "These two," states the *Handbook,* "shall be one flesh!"

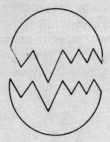

These constitute two different halves. Notice the "high points" and valleys are varied. They are arranged to make one complete whole!

Love brings opposites together for the purpose of supply and fulfillment. When we see this, *incompatibility* becomes a challenge. This often-charged ground for divorce turns out to be the key that opens the door to "living happily after."

As we move on to take up the challenge, please note again the halves in the above illustration. The high points represent the strong characteristics in personality—areas of strength, self-assurance, success. In between, however, are areas of inadequacy and personal need. These are what God wants to supply through our mate. This bringing together of strength to need—and need to strength—is the ultimate intention of God in marriage.

Then why should true love have its disagreements? Simply because after we have been pronounced *one* during the marriage ceremony, the becoming *one* in actuality has just begun. You now have ten . . . twenty . . . forty years to work out the pronouncement!

Due to misunderstanding and maladjustment, a couple can begin their marriage (and often this has been a part of their dating and engagement period) strong point to strong point. Both parties hesitate to "give in." The husband fears he may end up henpecked by a strong woman. The woman may cringe at the thought of being under a dictator. One who has known the free rein of single life hesitates

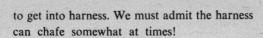

to get into harness. We must admit the harness can chafe somewhat at times!

Even after seeing something of God's great wisdom in giving you the mate you *need,* with the qualities you *lack,* it is possible to still feel that the partner needs changes before the ideal can be achieved. Being a dreamer, I began at once proclaiming, "Things are getting better!" To which my wife came back, "Really? Where?" I thought she was reacting negatively and she thought I had my head in the clouds. We decided to pray about the whole thing.

"Oh, God, change that woman," went up my impassioned plea.

From the next room came an equally sincere petition, "Oh, God, change that man You gave me."

Do you think God got confused? No. He just retired into the wings and left us on center stage to fight it out—willing to wait until He could get us quiet long enough to listen to His next revelation.

We have seen that when God gets two together, they are usually direct opposites in the *important* areas of operation—and for a specific reason.

If, for instance, money is the point of disagreement, adjustment is needed. One mate usually spends too much money and the other is apt to be frugal— *conflict!* "Honey, let's buy a new car." "We can't afford one now." "Well, let's paint the old one green." "You know very well I hate green cars." So it goes —one thing leads to another.

If there are children, another area of conflict can be the matter of discipline. One parent is too lenient —the other too strict. Needless battles have been fought on this with much resulting damage to the children. The day Judy and I finally made the adjustment here, our children rejoiced. Between their two parents they now have one balanced, adequate parent!

Are you beginning to see how these two halves fit together? Look at them joined as one—perfectly complementing each other. What computer could ever come up with that kind of answer?

3
Corporate Merger

Is this double talk: One plus one equals one—but it takes two? No—for here is the heart of the other two principles we are going to consider.

We have seen a couple truly wanting to be "one" —still feeling one or the other had to change. When realization dawned that God didn't expect either to change but make a spiritual adjustment—the whole thing fell into place. Husband, when you find out that in your wife you have everything you need to be an adequate man—and, wife, when you accept the fact that in your husband (or intended mate) you have all that is needed to make that "complete-ment"—then you will understand that marriage is more a *merger* than a partnership.

Suppose you buy a beautiful new, very-latest-model automobile. The initial investment is tremendous —but that is only the beginning. We all take it for granted that maintenance is part of the package. Regular changes of oil and lubrication are recommended by the manufacturer. Periodic checkups are needed to continuing good performance. Cars—no matter how new and beautiful—just do not keep in good condition without all of this proper attention. Marriage falls into this same category. Remember, marriage is *not* instant oneness!

In marriage husband and wife are so closely associated and their needs so interrelated that it is virtually impossible to separate them. But either one or the other can begin this necessary spiritual adjustment with the assurance that God had in mind the ultimate welfare of them both. Once you understand, accept, and put into practice this second principle, you can count upon results.

It was while teaching at a conference in Colombia, South America, that this second truth opened to me. My responsibility was to teach during the day and at night I found myself alone in my room weeping because I knew our marriag was not yielding the joy it should. As hard as we tried, Judy and I did not seem to be able to maintain the adjusting to one another that we knew was necessary. I kept asking within myself, "God, how do You take two stubborn personalities and make them into one person?" I turned the pages in my Bible to reread the familiar passage on marriage in 1 Peter, chapter 3, KJV. It begins with the word *Likewise*. . . . "Likewise, ye wives . . . Likewise, ye husbands. . . ." *Likewise* what? I found myself asking for the first time. What was Peter telling wives and husbands to be *like?*

Turning back to chapter 2, I found that servants were the subject of verses 18–20—and Christ was the example in verses 21–24. Shall we try to pick up Peter's reasoning about the marriage relationship?

> Servants, be subject [or submit] to your masters with all fear; not only to the good and gentle, but also to the froward [perverse ones]. For this is thankworthy, if a man for conscience toward God endure grief, suffering wrongfully. For what glory is it, if, when ye be buffeted for your faults, ye shall take it patiently? but if,

when ye do well and suffer for it, ye take it patiently, this is acceptable with God. For even hereunto were ye called, because Christ also suffered for us, leaving us an example, that ye should follow his steps: Who did no sin, neither was guile found in his mouth: Who, when he was reviled, reviled not again; when he suffered, he threatened not; but committed himself to him that judgeth righteously.

1 Peter 2:18–23 KJV

What was Peter saying? Just as servants were to submit—not only to good masters but to the ones who were hard, demanding and perverse; just as Jesus Christ did not revile back when He was reviled at, or threaten when He was threatened, but bore patiently the *unfair* suffering for us—*likewise* are husbands to dwell with their wives not just when they were nice and loving, but nagging, lazy, and perverse as well. *Likewise* were wives to submit to their husbands—not just when they were good or right, but when they were mean and demanding and perverse (1 Peter 3:1–7).

Well! I had been preaching about the need for wives to submit and husbands to love and yet had never understood these implications. I had known Christian wives who had agreed—in a measure—to Peter's words to wives, along with Paul's advice in Colossians 3:18; but they seemed to understand three important little words, "in the Lord," to mean *only* to submit to their husbands when they were "obedient to the Lord." This immediately left all Christian wives who had nonbelieving husbands free to judge their husband's spirituality before submitting. However,

25

this is a tragic misinterpretation of both Peter's and Paul's meaning.

First, examine with me Paul's statement in Colossians 3:18 from three different versions:

> Wives, submit yourselves unto your own husbands, as it is fit in the Lord. KJV

> Wives, be subject to your husbands—subordinate and adapt yourselves to them—as is right *and* fitting *and* your proper duty in the Lord. AMPLIFIED

> You wives, submit yourselves to your husbands, for that is what the Lord has planned for you. LB

Can you see that submitting to your husband is to be done as a "service to the Lord"? Your husband's relationship to the Lord has nothing to do with this. It is an attitude wives assume before God. As they do, He can take control and bring order where order is needed and change where change is needed.

Listen to Peter as he follows up his "likewise, wives":

> In like manner [as the slaves in 2:18–20] you married women, be submissive to your own husbands—subordinate yourselves as being secondary to and dependent on them, and adapt yourselves to them. So that even if any do not obey the Word [of God] they may be won over not by discussion but by the [godly] lives of their wives.
>
> 1 Peter 3:1 AMPLIFIED

(Do you catch "attitude" here? Submission becomes meaningless if it is attempted with a cold heart or resentful spirit.)

> When they observe the pure *and* modest way in which you conduct yourselves, together with your reverence [for your husband. That is, you are to feel for him all that reverence includes]—to respect, defer to, revere him; [revere means] to honor, esteem (appreciate, prize), and [in the human sense] adore him; [and adore means] to admire, praise, be devoted to, deeply love and enjoy [your husband]. v. 2

One wife told me at this point, "It revolutionized my thinking about submission when I realized that God wanted me to *enjoy* my husband! I had thought I could force myself to submit, obey, and adapt—but *enjoy*—that was impossible! It brought me to my knees. I realized I had to turn the whole thing over to God, confess my miserable failings, and ask him to make me *able* to enjoy my husband."

This underlines our utter dependence upon God. It is *His* process and no wife can submit to her husband in her own strength. It simply cannot be done. True submission can only come as she submits herself to God and asks that He take away any old fears, all selfishness and independence, and fill her instead with the love and joy that enables her to love and enjoy her husband. To better grasp this—taking into consideration both husband and wife (for they are intertwined in this tapestry called marriage)—we take one example from the Old Testament, and then several from my counseling files.

4
Sarah, Mother of Faith

We have long and loudly proclaimed Abraham as the Father of the Faith—and rightly so. But have you ever thought of the faith of his wife, Sarah? Peter says, in following up his words on submission:

> It was thus that Sarah obeyed Abraham (following his guidance and acknowledging his headship over her by) calling him lord —master, leader, authority. And you are her true daughters if you do right and let nothing terrify you—not giving way to hysterical fears or letting anxieties unnerve you.
>
> 1 Peter 3:6 AMPLIFIED

Now I have heard women say that Sarah didn't have anything to worry about—being married, as she was, to Abraham—this man of such great faith that he was chosen to become the father of Israel. Submitting to him ought to have been easy enough! But Peter refers to a time when it would have been much easier for Sarah to have given away to hysterical fears than to trust. As you read the background for this statement, you realize that Sarah's faith was far greater than Abraham's at times (Genesis 12:10–20).

On their journey from Haran to Canaan, they ran into a famine and Abraham decided to go down into

Egypt in order for his party to survive. Sarah was an unusually beautiful woman and Abraham thought the Egyptians might kill him in order to take his wife. So he said to Sarah:

"Honey, when we get down into Egypt, if anybody asks any questions, tell them that you are my sister."

Sarah didn't argue or tell Abraham what a cowardly thing she thought he was considering. She replied, "Yes, lord, I submit to you in faith. I believe God and trust Him."

Just as was feared, when they got to Egypt the word of Sarah's beauty reached the ears of Pharaoh and he sent his men to bring her to his house, having been told she was Abraham's sister.

When Sarah arrived at the harem of the King, don't you imagine that she fell on her face before God and claimed His protection since she had been obedient to her husband? And the voice of the Lord came to bear upon the king as he waited expectantly for this new addition to his harem. Through a series of plagues, the king realized something was wrong and upon learning that Sarah was Abraham's wife, he asked Abraham, "How come?" Abraham's answer was, "I was afraid. . . ."

No harm came to Sarah. Pharaoh understood that Abraham was a man of God and gave the party free access to continue on their journey.

Can you see that if you submit to your husband only when everything suits you, that doesn't take much faith? When your husband is the epitome of manliness, holiness, and everything else you want him to be, it is fairly easy to call him *Lord*. But Sarah submitted to Abraham even when she knew he was wrong. Wouldn't she have been justified in refusing to go along with his scheme? No, Sarah obeyed her husband and in so doing she was obedient to God and, therefore, was protected from all harm. Had she disobeyed, she would only have added her own disobedience to the disobedience of her husband, and the problem would have been compounded. Sarah wasn't trusting Abraham—she was trusting God and this faith moved the Hand of God. If God can impress a foreign and godless king, cannot He work in your marriage? Believe me, He can! But you see, you have to come under the biblical premise in order to have God get into the act. If you are going to fight your own battles—then God is going to let you fight your own battles!

But you ask, how far should I submit? My answer would be, according to your faith and not one bit more. Sarah was not afraid of the consequences of Abraham's act. She knew that as she submitted herself to her husband, God Almighty had to move in her behalf.

5
But, Does It Work Today?

This is a valid question and I want to give you some flesh and blood answers which are as up-to-date as tomorrow's newspaper.

Personal illustrations are expensive, but allow me to share one of my failures. In personality I am overt and aggressive. My wife is reserved and timid. One evening we entertained mutual friends. I monopolized the conversation with joy and eagerness. Several times I interrupted my wife's attempts to share or make her own quiet observations. Suddenly I was aware of her deep injury. This was not a new problem—but one I was having trouble conquering.

We said good-bye to our friends with contrived cheerfulness. I could feel the tension building. My trip to the airport with the friends took about an hour. As I drove home, I could see Judy's face with its hurt showing—and imagined her saying, "You really did it again tonight." I conjured my weak, but strongly stated defense, "Yes, but. . . ." I knew the words, *I'm sorry* wouldn't fit this time. I kept thinking I should have said something to her before I left —but I really hadn't known quite what to say.

As I parked the car I said, "Lord, I've done this thing so many times I am almost ashamed to repent again." I opened the front door with my insides churning and there she was—waiting for me. Her eyes were soft and so was her voice as she said, "Bob, while you were gone God showed me something."

(I thought it was going to go into the usual thing:
"You really hurt me."
"Yes, I know I did."
"Why?")

So I was all ready for her, and said, "Well. . . ." You know that defensive tone of voice we can assume when we aren't sure just what to say!

Her reply came with quietness and confidence, "I want you to know that I love you and you are my lord. God has shown me that He has made you head over me and over our family and this house—even when you are wrong."

My only words in answer to that were, "My Lord!" Standing there in the doorway something happened to me. It was frightening to be hit with the realization of what God had done and where He had placed me. Looking at my wife and the love in her eyes, I knew that I was responsible for her and everyone else under my roof. It was an awesome moment and inside something melted and faded away. A bit of the stubborn pride and self-reliance of Bob Mumford died there on the threshhold. I knew the only way I could be head of my wife and household was for me to submit, obey, and trust in *my* head, Jesus Christ.

The principle was working. My wife submitted to me even when we both knew I had been wrong. Her submission opened the way for God to deal directly with me in force. If Judy had reacted in the usual way instead of doing what God told her, we would have been forced into argument and disagreement—each up his separate tree.

Wives, when you have faith to say to your husband, "You are my head—you are the master of my house—I want to submit to you," then you are obeying God's command and God is free to deal with your husband.

We are not talking about manipulation. This does not work. You cannot make a deal with God and say you will submit so that God can make your husband into the kind of person you want him to be. Remember Peter said you are "to love him, respect him, admire him and *enjoy* him." This is God's plan for you as a wife. God knows you will be happier enjoying your husband than you would be scheming and manipulating in order to make him different—according to *your* specifications.

I have heard wives say, "Mr. Mumford, you just cannot imagine how unreasonable my husband is." That's right, I may not know all the circumstances, but God knows. That is one reason why He gave us the extreme example of Abraham who told his wife to say she was his sister, permitting her to be taken to the king's harem. And did you know that Abraham did this not just once, but a second time? Read Genesis chapter 20 and see a repeat performance of the Egyptian episode. Yet God intended to make Abraham the father of many nations—a man of great faith and responsibility. God certainly wants to make your husband the patriarch of your house. Are you willing to submit to His plan with the faith of Sarah?

Following up my own experience, here are some other Today workings of God in establishing His divine order in our homes.

Twenty years is a big investment to make in any venture, but one woman came to me for counseling with the story of two decades of married life, viewing it as a complete failure. She had faithfully prayed (her husband was not a Christian); she had quoted Bible verses and left little tracts and other reminders around where he could not miss them—all to no avail. Her husband was an alcoholic with horse racing another of his main interests. The breach between them was ever-widening. This interview came shortly after Judy and I had witnessed God's workings in our lives.

"Are you willing to try something God has been showing me?" I asked. She replied that if it were in the Bible and I recommended it, she would, at least, be willing to listen.

Turning to Peter's words to wives, I concluded with, "Are you willing to submit to your husband as Peter is describing?"

"But my husband isn't even a Christian—submission would mean nothing to him."

"I realize that, but it says here to submit anyway. Can you do it in faith?"

This was a big step in faith (and in such a surprising direction!) that she asked for a week to consider it.

The following week she returned, saying she was ready to give it a try. I then asked, "Now can you think of something your husband has asked you to do but you have refused?"

"Yes. He continues to ask me to go with him to the racetrack, knowing that I won't. You know I couldn't go there."

"Why not?" I queried. (Let me pause and say that I am not advocating racetrack indulgences as a way of life!)

"Well, I don't like racetracks—horses—or the people who go there. Besides they gamble and that's against the Word of God."

"The racetrack may not be a nice place to go," I said, "but neither was Pharaoh's harem. Can you believe God will take care of you wherever you go as long as you go in obedience to His will?" The answer was a hesitant *yes,* punctuated with a question mark. About a month later she returned with this account.

The usual invitation had come from her husband and she replied, "Yes, dear, I think I'd like to go with you tomorrow."

Openmouthed, he exploded, "But you can't do that!"

"I promise not to embarrass you or your friends —I'll just go along and enjoy myself."

After a long silence the still unbelieving question came, "Are you serious?"

You see, resistance had been going on so long— and had become so strong—that it had become a way of life for them. The husband then took a deep breath and said, "OK, and while we're at it, I might as well tell you something: Last week I bought a racing horse."

Receiving this news took special faith. Catching *her* breath, the wife replied smilingly, "How nice. I'd like to meet him."

Saturday came and dressed in an outfit of her husband's liking, off they went. Three Saturdays in a row they went to the racetrack. She found horses did have a certain beauty when you looked at them through the eyes of love. And her husband was finding out some things looked better, too!

The third Sunday morning, the man of the house surprised everyone by saying, "If you can go to the racetrack, I reckon I can go to church." (Are you ahead of me and guessing the outcome?) Yes, it only took a few Sundays before God was able to work in that man's life and he made a commitment to Christ as His Saviour.

After twenty years of apartness, one partner's obedience (in this case, the wife's daring to yield to her husband in faith), permitted the warmth and light of God's love to flow from one to the other. God's promise inherent at the beginning of their marriage, "These two shall be one," became a reality.

Another incident shows us how a person can do good and still be tragically wrong. There is a fine line of obedience for each of us and we must be discerning to be able to discover it. Many, many women go to church against their husbands' wishes. They sing in the choir, teach Sunday school, attend prayer meetings, visit the sick and elderly. All these things are good and need to be done. But they are wrong for *you* if your husband would rather have you home. God wants someone to do all those worthy things in the church. He needs someone to sing and teach and visit the sick—but first of all He wants you to submit to your husband. *This is your first priority*. Then if God wants you to do some work for Him, He will impress the idea on your husband.

A woman of my acquaintance has a beautiful singing voice. She is often asked to sing in church or at other meetings. Her husband prefers she stay home most of the time as they have several small children. Once I asked her, "How is your ministry of singing coming along?"

Her smiling reply was, "I am finally learning to sing only when God wants me to."

"Well, how do you know when He does and doesn't want you to sing?" I countered.

She laughed and her answer was one of assurance

and joy. "God has given me a husband as a head. I just ask Jim. If he says *no,* I know God doesn't want me to sing. If Jim says *yes,* I feel certain the Lord wants to use me and my voice. It is so simple and works so beautifully."

Many women take on the spiritual leadership of their homes because they feel it is their duty to do so. But this is not what the Word of God has to say to wives. This is leadership by default—because the husband didn't, the wife did. God's desire is to restore leadership to its intended source.

Here is one more Today story which shows God's workings.

A wife tells it this way: "My husband was not a Christian. Had I left it up to Tom there would not have been any Bible reading or prayers at bedtime with the children—or any church attendance. I wanted to submit to my husband but felt I could not until he was 'ready.' One day a real problem came into our family. One of the children was caught smoking marijuana in the school parking lot.

"I was numbed—blaming my husband because he had not taken his place as spiritual head of the house with the result of no proper authority or discipline. I went to God and cried, 'I'm sorry I tried to take Tom's place as head of this house. If you have made him my head, I'm not going to play that role anymore. I am sick and tired to being responsible for the children. I am stepping down right now, God, and if You want something done about this situation, You'll have to make Tom do it!'

"When Tom came home from work and was told about the incident, he asked, 'Well, what are you going to do about it?' 'Nothing. I have finally realized that you are head of this house.'

"I had a good night's sleep and upon awaking next

morning found Tom walking the floor with the evidence of a sleepless night on his face. He admitted that he had spent most of the hours reviewing his lack of responsibility for the children, along with his desire to remedy the situation in the future—even to the point of assuring me that he wanted to join us in attending church and participating in family worship. Clearing his throat, he said, 'I'm not at all sure I believe God is who the Bible makes Him out to be, but I think our children should know what it says and make up their own minds about it.' "

This wife had hesitated years before stepping aside because she thought her spiritual leadership was better than nothing. In reality, the wrong leadership is worse than no leadership at all. When a wife abdicates the throne in the house and accepts the role God has created for her—and created her to fulfill—God will fill the vacuum at the top with the proper head and authority. The wife does not submit to her husband because she thinks he is strong and trustworthy in his own right, but because she believes that God will lead the family through her husband. She is fitting in with God's order for marriage. Remember Sarah was not trusting Abraham to get her out of that harem—she was trusting God!

All of these incidents have been told as the wife has presented the problems. It seems that women are more willing to seek help when it is needed. Could this be why God said first, "Likewise, wives. . ."? Following is just a brief checklist in case some wife is still experiencing difficulty in understanding, accepting, or putting into operation the principle we have been discussing.

6
If It Isn't Working....

When submission just does not seem to work, there are several vital observations that must be made.

First: Remember, God's law stands firm. He is never wrong, neither has He changed His mind for you—or in your particular situation.

Second: Reexamine your submission for areas of manipulation, self-sacrifice, or even a false martyrdom.

Third: Your submission must be toward God, in pure faith, that He will intervene in your situation. Submission is *to* your husband, but it is *unto* God, expecting Him to do what otherwise cannot be done.

Fourth: When authority is released by the wife, and has not been taken up by the husband, great care must be exercised to trust God for the children and stand firmly upon your convictions.

Fifth: Remember your goal is to *submit* and *enjoy* your husband, not try to change him. Submission without results is evidence that you have missed the *spirit* of submission and need to repeat the lessons.

7
Instant Leadership

Why must the wife submit even when her husband is not actively involved in seeking God's way in their marriage? Does this mean that men are privileged persons who can get away with irresponsible behavior? Of course not! In God's Book, nobody gets away with anything. God intends to deal with every husband as much as He desires to work with the wives.

When a woman obeys God and submits to her husband, God can deal directly with him. Ever hear of interference in a football game? Get the idea? When the wife tries to deal with her husband on her own, she interferes in God's dealings by her disobedience. The reason for this order becomes clear when we take another look at the biblical picture of marriage. God says that He intended to take two opposites, a man and a woman, and make them into *one* person. One person only has *one* head and the Bible states plainly *who* is to function as head.

> But I would have you know, that the head of every man is Christ; and the head of the woman is the man; and the head of Christ is God.
>
> 1 Corinthians 11:3 KJV

But there is one matter I want to remind you about: that a wife is responsible to her

husband, her husband is responsible to
Christ, and Christ is responsible to God.

This order explains why Sarah was safe when she
submitted to her husband even when he was wrong.
Over all is God's responsibility and love for us. It is
like an umbrella of protection and guidance. As long
as we stay within its covering, submit to the one who
is our head, we are safe.

We mentioned that there is no instant "oneship."
However, there is instant "headship." The husband
becomes the head of his wife at the time they repeat
their vows. We have to grow into oneness, but husbands do not grow into headship. They are placed in
that position by God right from the start. Often a
man does not know he is head of his wife and their
home; others do not act as if they were the heads—
but that does not change God's ordered setup. Wife,
don't sit around and wait for your husband to become
"spiritual" enough to be your head—he *is* your head.
When you act as if he were, God has a way of bringing
the full force of the responsibility to his attention.

No man can say to his wife, "Look, it says in the
Bible you are to *obey* me," without seeing what follows: "Husbands, *love* your wives!" Remember what
we said earlier? This is a great mystery and Satan is
out to keep it that way! Read the following words
with a prayer for understanding—for they are meant
to be understood.

And you husbands, show the same kind of
love to your wives as Christ showed to the
church when he died for her. . . . That is
how husbands should treat their wives, lov-

41

ing them as parts of themselves. For since a man and his wife are now one, a man is really doing himself a favor and loving himself when he loves his wife! No one hates his own body, but lovingly cares for it, just as Christ cares for his body the church, of which we are parts. . . . So again I say, a man must love his wife as part of himself; and the wife must see to it that she deeply respects her husband—obeying, praising and honoring him.

Ephesians 5:25–30,33

You wives, submit yourselves to your husbands, for this is what the Lord has planned for you. And you husbands must be loving and kind to your wives and not bitter against them, nor harsh.

Colossians 3:18,19

Christ is the pattern for husbands. Not only *what* he does, but *how* he does it. This is what Peter was referring to when he wrote: "Likewise, ye husbands dwell with your wives. . ." (1 Peter 3:7). Just as servants were to obey, not only their good masters, but their mean and perverse ones, likewise as Christ reviled not back when He was reviled; likewise as wives were to submit to their husbands—good and bad—*likewise* are husbands to love their wives—not only the sweet and kind ones—but the nagging, pouting, selfish ones as well.

That's the first command, husbands. Love as Christ loves. Don't answer back when you are being nagged at. Don't retaliate when you're being needled. Love those who distrust you, misunderstand you, fight you. Exactly like that, Peter said, are husbands to dwell with their wives. Listen to this same verse (1 Peter 3:7) from the Amplified Bible: "In the same manner you married men should live considerately with [your wives] with an intelligent recognition [of the marriage relation]. . . ."

When I first realized that God was in the process of making one whole person out of the stubborn personalities of Judy and myself, I thought, "How wonderful!" Then I began to understand more about God's intention and ended up saying, "Help! I'm responsible for my wife!" As the head of my wife, I have an awesome responsibility in the eyes of God. Christ was placed as head of the church and given authority over her. Just so, says the Bible, have I been placed as head of my wife and given authority over her.

In our day and culture a statement like that may sound strange. With Women's Lib receiving such a warm reception from many—with reams of printed propaganda pouring off the presses promoting this idea—with boys and girls being taught to think alike, look alike, act alike, and that marriage is an agreement between two equally independent and responsible parties—what chance does our *Manufacturer's Handbook* have? It has withstood centuries of come-and-go ideas and I believe it will stand on its own two feet and continue to explain how things were intended to work and the consequences of *not* doing it this way.

The principle of headship is a fundamental one in marriage. Much of our confusion in families today comes from a violation of this basic order. We have shared illustrations about the consequences of a wife's refusal to follow God's ordained order. There are also serious consequences for the husband who does not exercise the authority God has placed in him.

In the Book of Numbers, chapter 30, Moses instructed Israel concerning this matter:

> The Lord has commanded that when anyone makes a promise to the Lord, either to do something or to quit doing something, that vow must not be broken: the person must do exactly as he has promised.
>
> v.1

This rule was always binding on men and on women who were divorced or widowed, said Moses, but there is an exception for a daughter who lived in her father's house or a wife who lived in her husband's house.

> . . . [If] her husband [or father] hears of [the vow] and says nothing, the vow shall stand [and she must do it]; but if he refuses to allow it on the first day he hears of it, her vow is void and Jehovah will forgive her. So her husband may [has the authority] to either confirm or nullify her vow.
>
> vs. 10–13

The consequences of this arrangement follow:

> . . . but if he says nothing for a day, then he has already agreed to it. If he waits more than a day and then refuses to permit the vow, whatever penalties to which she agreed [whatever promises she made]

44

shall come upon him—he shall be responsible.

vs. 14,15

This principle stated many thousands of years ago
is still in operation. It is what Paul and Peter were referring to two thousands years ago when they talked
about headship. It is in effect, too, for every husband
today.

It means that if your wife comes home and says
she promised to teach Sunday school or sing in the
choir or cook for the church supper, and you think
this is a rash promise, you are to tell her so—in love.
It might go something like this: "Honey, I think you
promised more than you can handle. We need you
here at home." If she tells you she made the promise
to the Lord, you are to say, "Yes, I know, but the
Lord won't hold you to it, because I am your head
and refuse to give you permission."

This is exercising your authority as Christ exercises
His authority over us. He tells us what we are to do.
But notice that Christ never *forces* us to obey. We
still have our choice of obedience or rebellion. The
consequences are ours. A husband is responsible for
telling his wife what she is to do, but it is her responsibility to obey. If she chooses to ignore him, the consequences come upon her. The authority of the husband does not include the right to force his wife into
obedience. Here is the difference between a head and
a tyrant.

In most homes today the husband may possibly
have a final say-so in major decisions, but in the rou-
tine of daily living, Mom is head of the house. Who
decides if Anne should take dancing lessons—or if

Johnny should join the cub scouts? Who usually pays the bills and signs the report card when it is below a *C* average? Who accepts the invitation to an evening out or invites the pastor for dinner? From the husband's point of view, this may seem the easy way to live. The wife may be an efficient organizer, handling everything so well that he doesn't really need to do anything except to grunt acquiescence from behind his evening newspaper. Headship isn't easy and may not be desired, but it is essential if two are to become one in marriage and if the family is to mature spiritually.

No husband can become the head of his wife in its full meaning without recognizing that Christ is *his* head. No man can love a woman as Christ loves us without yielding himself fully to Christ. Paul wrote several times that the mystery of the Christian life is that Christ lives *in* us. By nature we are selfish, stubborn, and unloving, except as it suits our whims and needs. We must call upon Christ in order to properly love each other.

It may be easy for me to act in love toward my neighbors, friends, or the people whom I counsel; but when I am at home and faced with a wife who forgets to iron the shirt I want to wear—or children who interrupt my study time, then I have to come to my knees and confess that I don't know how to love those God has given me to love at home. At times I don't know how to exercise my authority in love—yet I *know* this is my first responsibility to God.

Yes, headship has its demands. But headship must also come before a man is ready to be used as a leader in the Christian community. Listen to Paul on this subject:

46

Now a bishop (superintendent, overseer)
. . . must be the husband of one wife . . . .
He must rule his own household well,
keeping his children under control, with
true dignity, commanding their respect in
every way and keeping them respectful.
For if a man does not know how to rule his
own household, how is he to take care of
the church of God? . . . Let deacons be
the husbands of but one wife, and let them
manage their children and their households
well.

1 Timothy 3:2,4,5,12 AMPLIFIED

Listen to this joint report on some "headship" adjustment in one family. It was only after fifteen years of bickering and blundering that these two came to realize what God had to say about headship and submission.

HUSBAND   We were both strong-willed and stubborn.
We both had to learn to yield—I to Christ, and
my wife to me. We had to ask God to change
our habits of thinking and reacting. My wife
wanted to submit, but she was so used to questioning most of my ideas that her reaction was
automatic. I was so used to anticipating her reaction that I often did not exercise my authority
because I honestly wanted to avoid conflict. And
we both suffered the consequences. However,
slowly we learned to react to Christ instead of to
each other.

WIFE   I had been a Christian some years before my
husband and had assumed leadership for the
children's spiritual guidance both at church and

at home. I realized that I was usurping my husband's authority in many areas, but to change the whole thing around was easier said than done. I wanted desperately to do the right thing, but something in me reacted almost violently to my husband's decisions. I knew I was wrong and usually ended up on my knees crying to God about it. If my husband told me I couldn't go to prayer meeting as I always had, I cried and said I thought the Lord wanted me to go. Deep down inside I knew my husband was right, but I tried to influence his decisions anyhow.

HUSBAND Watching my wife's tears was the hardest part. I asked the Lord if He really did want us to stay home from prayer meeting and the direction seemed a clear *yes*. Until then, most of our Christian activities had been church-centered. Now, as a family, God seemed to want us to become Christ-centered at home as well. I was tempted to give in to my wife's tears but knew if I did I would not be exercising the authority God had entrusted to me. The turning point came one night when I asked my wife not to go to a certain group meeting to which she was accustomed to going each month. I had prayed about it and felt she should not go that particular night. She reacted rather violently and asked if I were going to force her to stay home. I told her, of course not. She then asked if I would pray for her if she went anyhow. Again, I told her I always prayed for her welfare. But I told her I would rather she not go without my permission.

WIFE I recall snapping back, "Why don't you give it then?" and left the house in a huff. I told myself my husband was just being silly and was going too far. At first everything seemed as usual—chatting, sewing, having refreshments. Then I began to sense something was different, although I could not put my finger on what it was. I was uncomfortable—as if I had stepped from a warm, secure place into the cold dark outside. I actually seemed chilly listening to the flow of the conversation. Suddenly I realized the conversation had become gossip about the family life of a mutual friend. I squirmed in my seat and was not enjoying myself as usual. I left early and couldn't get home quickly enough, realizing I had learned a valuable lesson. In disobeying my husband, I had stepped out from the protective covering of God's love—I was out of order!

No, headship and submission aren't things we can learn once for all, any more than Christian maturity is something we come into once for all. Both involve a daily contact with God. There comes to the husband who is yielding to Christ an attitude, an authority that is never abusive—a firmness that is love in action—a strength that never violates the one who is under his authority—just as Christ never violates our personalities. This kind of loving authority never takes advantage of another.

A woman who yields to God by submitting to her husband finds that this never leads to a loss of true liberty. One wife said, "The more I am able to submit, the greater the freedom I experience." This is not just clever religious double-talk. It is the way the process is meant to work. A locomotive is free to perform to the limit of its potential as long as it stays on the tracks. Off the tracks, it is hopelessly stuck. True liberation for a woman is when she is free to function to the full potential for which she was created.

In this connection, I want to present a verse of instruction and suggestion in three translations—1 Peter 3:7:

> Likewise, ye husbands, dwell with them according to knowledge. . . .
>
> KJV

> You husbands must be careful of your wives, being thoughtful of their needs and honoring them as the weaker sex. . . .
>
> LB

> Similarly, you husbands should try to understand the wives that you live with, honoring them as physically weaker. . . .
>
> PHILLIPS

It is clear from the context that when Peter speaks of "knowing" wives, he means two kinds of knowledge—the knowledge of what the marriage relationship means, and the knowledge of who the wife is and what she needs. A common failing among us husbands is that we don't know our wives' needs. Consequently we are not able to love them as they long to be loved.

One day in a barber shop, a magazine cover caught my eye. Picking it up to while away my waiting time, I saw headlined, HOW TO RECOGNIZE LOVE-STARVED WOMEN. The article was talking about sex-starved women, but it is really a tragic fact that many wives are starved for love within the marriage relationship. They truly want to be able to love their husbands as they should. God puts the responsibility for initiating love on the husband. Wives are told to submit first—husbands are told to love first. Interesting?

In fifteen years as a minister, I have counseled thousands of couples. It has made me realize that most women operate on only a small percentage of their capacity to love. They are shut up—drawn into themselves—waiting for their husbands to bring about that liberty they desire in their marriage.

Husbands, God tells us to love our wives. Learn to *know her*. Remember Peter's "Likewise . . . ." You are to love her with her bad habits (when she forgets to sort your socks—serves hamburgers for dinner four days in a row—forgets to fill up the gas tank in your car). Love her when she argues, complains, or cries to get her way.

If you aren't yet aware of her needs, ask God to show you. You will soon discover things about your wife you never knew before. She may be longing for you to take her hand and walk around the block after supper, or she may be tired from carrying the baby and want to have her back rubbed. Little things or big things—find things that tell her that you care.

You do realize, don't you, that you are not to love them in order for them to change? That isn't love—that is manipulation! Our words to wives about manipulation go for husbands as well. If she never changes, you are still to love her. You are to love her because of who she is—your wife—and you need her. When you do, you will discover you enjoy it a great deal more than when you complained and wished she would change. We love because it is God's command.

When a husband begins to love his wife like that —"according to knowledge"—something happens in her. In your wife there comes that same motivation that is present in your loving. Soon the wife is motivated to be to you the kind of wife you want. She finds herself wanting to be everything to you that she possibly can be. As you reach out, she responds.

We talked earlier about the maintenance and upkeep on a new car. In thinking about the response of a woman to a man, the comparison of "sowing and reaping" and cultivation of a beautiful garden seems more appropriate. Men, what we sow—we reap. Sow neglect of her and soon it brings forth the fruit of her neglect of you. Threats and bribes cannot correct this situation. Continued harshness produces a harvest which is also evident in a hardened atmosphere in the entire home. Children are aware of what is going on. Seeds have a way of producing a crop of like kind.

But as seeds of deep desire and fulfillment are sown the crop takes on a different pattern. Like brings forth like. Watered and cultivated and warmed, she becomes more desirable than ever before. Joyfully she says with the Shulamite maiden in the Song of Solomon, "I am my beloved's and I am the one he desires" (7:10).

8
Fringe Benefits

This generally accepted phrase is well known in our business dealings. God has many fringe benefits resulting from this oneness He has ordained. Two are mentioned by Peter:

> . . .[realizing that you] are joint heirs of the grace (God's unmerited favor) of life, in order that your prayers may not be hindered and cut off.—Otherwise you cannot pray effectively.
>
> 1 Peter 3:7 AMPLIFIED

> . . . if you don't treat her as you should, your prayers will not get ready answers.
>
> LB

First, there is an aspect of life that can never be discovered or experienced until a man and woman come together and enjoy this joining together as one. It is a joint inheritance God has reserved for them. It cannot be experienced or inherited by one individual alone, or in marriages where there is no knowledge of or interest in God's plan in His instituted arrangement for completeness. He wants us to be "joint heirs of life."

When Judy and I began to adjust to one another according to God's plan, this promise became alive to us. When our union became communion, we began to touch and know a form of earthly relationship that contains more joys and satisfactions than most people can imagine. Most of us have had glimpses of it at times—but God meant this to be a way of life!

When resentments, friction, fighting stops—when the husband loves his wife with the love of Christ and the wife submits to her husband in faith—there is a unity established that defies the elements of a hostile society with its swinging and dealing and defying of God's laws. Can you imagine God's joy and His consequent response to marital unity and happiness in the midst of present confusion! We have experienced His approbation and a literal opening of the "storehouse of heaven" for spiritual, physical, and financial blessing.

Our second fringe benefit lies in the area of answered prayers. Remember how the Living Bible puts it: "If you don't treat her [your wife] as you should, your prayers will not get ready answers." There have been times in my own life when I have pounded the doors of heaven and decided God must be out of town. Then would come a voice, "Mumford, you had better get together with your wife—remember?" As we cultivate oneness in spirit, God answers prayers in a most remarkable way. Your children, your finances, your sex life—all parts of your life will know it! We are "heirs together" and we have a prayer-answering service available that far outshines any fringe benefit from any other investment we could possibly make. But it takes two of us: "These two shall be one flesh."

9
The Thirty-Day Plan

Thirty-Day Plan? Yes, try it God's way for thirty days. Whether you are in the planning stages for your marriage—if you are on your honeymoon—if you've been married ten years or twenty—if this is your first or third attempt—will you consider giving it a try *His Way?* This may be the first time you have been exposed to these three divine principles—or you may have a nodding acquaintance with them. You may even have given them a brief try but never been totally sold on the idea. Let me tell you—one and all—I believe a thirty-day trial will bring results that will surprise you and reward every effort.

To those of you who are just launching out onto the sea of matrimony, I would ask that you read (together, if possible) these biblical principles again and again. Discuss them and pray about them. Go into your marriage with your eyes wide open to the glorious possibilities waiting for you. Most couples consider finances—where they want to live—if the wife should work—what about children. Please put these three principles—your mate's supply of your own inadequacies, headship, submission—at the top of your list and watch the other problems fall into solution.

To those who have been wondering if marriage is still a valid way of life, I hope I have given you some food for thought.

And to those of you who are up your separate

trees at this time, how about coming down and considering with me—and each other—the possibilities of forsaking your own little fenced-off NO TRESPASSING areas and reaching out to new horizons?

I've heard times without number: "I won't come down unless she comes down first!" (And the same response from party of the second part.) ". . . For twenty years she has been nagging and suspicious and independent." (Reply to that one: "For twenty years I've kept house and cared for the children—with never a word of thanks.") Sound familiar to you?

If you are up separate trees, which one of you has the more faith? One of you has to let your guard down, trust God, and step in His direction.

Husband, do you see that God has given you this woman to love? Can you see that you are responsible for her? She may not be perfect. There may be something within you that rises in rebellion when she starts —pick, pick, pick—or taking over the reins. May I say that this is part of divine order. Men, we are created with a built-in automatic response to the plan God has ordained in headship. When we react adversely to usurpation, this is part of our defense mechanism. We are at our intended best when we operate within divine guidelines.

Most men, when they begin to look at their wives as they really are, will find themselves saying, "God, I understand that You have given her all of the things that I really need. If it were not for her, I don't know where I would be today." At least this has been my experience. The trouble is that we don't stop long enough to evaluate our situations.

God says, "Love her. She is part of you. If you don't know how to love her, ask Me. I will teach you how."

Wife, do you have the faith to submit to your husband—respect, love, and enjoy him? Submit as far as your faith permits and ask God to replenish your supply when it runs short! My wife has learned to submit to me. Deep down in her being she submits, even when I am wrong. I know it and it frightens me. Before she used to object and tried to make me see my error. I argued back and 'round and 'round we went. Now as she submits, God brings the full force of what I am doing right home to me.

Wife, do you think submission is asking too much? Do you think God would ask more than He intends to give you ability to undertake for Him?

It makes no difference who you are, where you are, how much you have been hurt, or retaliated in return. If you submit to God as sincerely as you know how, and submit to each other according to the principles we have shared—husband and wife—your marriage can become something "out of this world." For God takes the things of the world and makes them into things eternal. Christ died to make this possible. He died to make it possible for us to experience the healing of our relationships. He wants to impart His wholeness to complete the "whole" of God's Words given to man at the very beginning of time, as we know time.

> And the Lord God said, it isn't good for
> man to be alone; I will make a companion
> for him, a helper suited to his needs . . .
> and the two become one person.
> Genesis 2:18,24

Living happily ever after? This is my prayer.

The content of this book is available on audio and video cassette from:

PO Box 22341
Fort Lauderdale
Florida 33315

"Please, Bob Mumford, Tell Them It Works...."

Perhaps nothing more clearly demonstrates what we've been talking about than this letter from a lady in Maryland.

My dear Bob Mumford:

I just can't stop thanking God for your tape on marriage. I feel Jesus wants you to know what's been happening in our family.

I am thirty-nine years old and for sixteen years I was taking drugs and then turned to alcohol. My husband Ed was also an alcoholic who started drinking when he was thirteen years old. We have seven sons, aged 21, 19, 17, 16, 14, 13, and 11½.

Four years ago we came into a fellowship of people with a similar problem and my husband sobered up right away. Unfortunately I wasn't able to believe that there was a power greater than myself who could help me. With the liquor and the pills I also suffered bouts of depression and surges of compulsive hatred towards my sons, my husband, and myself. I tried to kill myself about eleven times by using barbiturates, paregoric, and overdoses of aspirin. Several times I ended up at the emergency room, and my psychiatrist told me I had consumed enough pills to kill a horse. Ed who works as a longshoreman had to call me on the phone every day just to see if the kids and I were OK.

After two years of meetings with others with a similar problem I finally tried to sober up. For five months I hung on for dear life, barely surviving the increasing pressure of depression and the urge to drink. I knew it was just a matter of time before I would have to start drinking again.

One night when I was feeling lousy, I happened to turn the television set to a Billy Graham Crusade. I listened to Dr. Graham telling how this Man Jesus Christ had died for all of our sicknesses, our sins, our hatred, and our evil desires. He had died to pay our debt and to set us free. All we had to do was to turn ourselves over to Him. As I listened I realized that my eyes were running over with tears. Three of our boys were in the living room with me. Steve looked at my tears and walked out of the room to hide his embarrassment. The other two obviously felt sorry for me, and when I fell to my knees, they knelt with me. We had never prayed together before, but now all three of us asked Jesus to come into our lives and help us. Before the program was over, Steve had joined us on his knees too.

That, Mr. Mumford, was the beginning. Slowly but surely Jesus became more real in our home. He delivered me from my hatred and I began to learn how to love. Soon my husband and our other sons asked Jesus into their lives as well.

We were sober, and we prayed together, but things were still not right in our household. We were old hands at fighting and cursing and tempers often flared. I am afraid I was the cause of most of the trouble. I was so proud of my lasting sobriety and newfound freedom from the urge to drink that I began to consider myself a super-spiritual Christian. I quoted Bible verses and told my family how to behave until my husband started calling me "Sergeant" or "Sister."

Then one evening at the fellowship meeting I had been attending I stood up to speak and told how I had learned to be self-confident and to stand up for my rights. I firmly believed that no human being could tell me what to do or not to do. No one but Jesus could order me around, I thought.

After my little talk, a friend came up to me and said he had a tape I might want to hear. I was always eager to hear teaching tapes, and said, "Sure, I want to hear it." He brought it over to my house the next day, and I sat there, gritting my teeth, listening to you tell wives they ought to submit to their husbands. I wanted to shut you up until you started talking about what the husband needs to do, then I wanted to play the tape for Ed. I thought he needed to learn a thing or two about being a better husband!

I played the tape that night for Ed, and he grinned from ear to ear through the entire part dealing with the wives. Then it was my turn to grin and he grew thoughtful while you talked to the husbands. Before the tape was over we were grinning at each other, then laughing, then crying a little and before it was over, Jesus brought us together in prayer. In my heart I *knew* I *wanted* to submit to Ed.

Right away Ed told me I couldn't do this and I couldn't do that, and the first few days and weeks were hell. But I *wanted* to do the right thing, and every day while Ed was gone to work, I listened to your tape again, read my Bible and prayed. I was too stubborn to submit myself, but little by little Jesus worked a miracle in me. He's changing me inside, and I can only praise Him. Things are so different now. I'm so much happier, and it's getting better every day. Ed knows I will submit to him, and he also knows he is responsible to Jesus. Our children know the difference, and our seventeen-year-old who was ashamed to show his emotions before God, now has come to Jesus. I have heard him tell that he is proud of his parents.

The day I decided to submit to my husband marked a turning point in our lives as a Christian family. We've begun to experience a new and deeper happiness. The relationships in the family are changing and growing better. The sparks aren't flying like they used to, and trouble areas and problems are coming to the light and being healed one-by-one. And I'm a lot happier than the woman who stood up in front of that group and said she'd learned to stand up for her rights!

Our finances are affected as well. Ed's work has doubled and four of our boys have told us they want no money for themselves except of course some little spending money. The two oldest who are in the Navy send their allotments home. The other two bring their entire paychecks. God is really taking care of us.

The changes are so wonderful, Bob Mumford. I wish you could see our seven boys. Every one of them filled with the love of Jesus, eager to tell their friends about the difference He makes in a life. Steve was a long-haired hippy who wore sunglasses and a leather jacket to school. The teachers complained about his influence on other students and we had to take him out of the eleventh grade. Today he is in the Navy. He was next to being honor boy in boot camp, made the highest average (95) in jet mechanics' school. Then he felt the Lord leading him to go into cook's school where he averaged highest (95–97) in his course and is coming up for third class rank. He tells us: "I don't take the credit, Jesus is doing it all!"

It's been five months since we heard

your tape and I asked Jesus to help me submit to my husband. Everything in our household is falling into place so beautifully. I'm far from the perfect, submissive wife, but it is wonderful to watch God working in our family.

Please, Bob Mumford, tell others it really works. I'm not proud of the mess our lives were in, but I praise God for the miracle He is working in our house. Friends tell us that our faces radiate joy, and that we are so different. It is all Jesus! I can't wait for each new day to see what Jesus has in store for us.

I know what it is to be high on drugs and alcohol. But nothing, believe me, *nothing* can come close to what it is like to be with Jesus.

> God bless you.
> Yours in Jesus.
> Flo